SCIENCE PUZZLES for Clever Kids

Puzzles and solutions
by Damara Strong

M.S

and Dr Gareth Moore

B.Sc (Hons) M.Phil Ph.D

Illustrations and cover
artwork by Chris Dickason

Designed by Zoe Bradley

☆

Edited by Susannah Bailey

☆

Cover design by Angie Allison

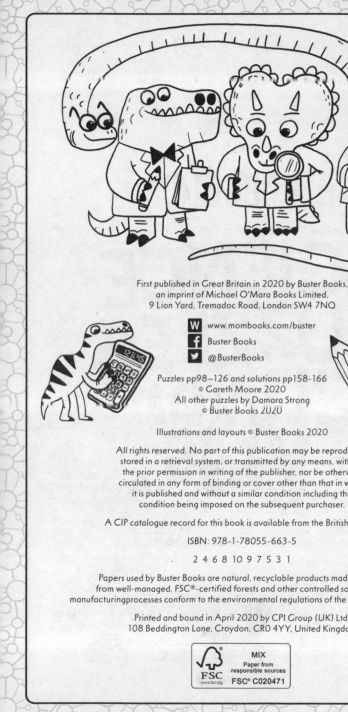

First published in Great Britain in 2020 by Buster Books,
an imprint of Michael O'Mara Books Limited,
9 Lion Yard, Tremadoc Road, London SW4 7NQ

W www.mombooks.com/buster
f Buster Books
🐦 @BusterBooks

Puzzles pp98–126 and solutions pp158–166
© Gareth Moore 2020
All other puzzles by Damara Strong
© Buster Books 2020

Illustrations and layouts © Buster Books 2020

A CIP catalogue record for this book is available from the British Library.

ISBN: 978-1-78055-663-5

2 4 6 8 10 9 7 5 3 1

Papers used by Buster Books are natural, recyclable products made of wood
from well-managed, FSC®-certified forests and other controlled sources. The
manufacturingprocesses conform to the environmental regulations of the country of origin.

Printed and bound in April 2020 by CPI Group (UK) Ltd,
108 Beddington Lane, Croydon, CR0 4YY, United Kingdom

MIX
Paper from
responsible sources
FSC® C020471
FSC
www.fsc.org

INTRODUCTION

Get ready for a scientific adventure with this exciting book that's packed full of puzzles. Work your way through over 100 puzzles, all designed to test your knowledge of STEM subjects (STEM stands for Science, Technology, Engineering and Maths). Each puzzle can be tackled on its own and you can work through the book at your own pace.

At the top of every page, there is a space for you to write how much time it took you to complete the puzzle. Don't be afraid to make notes on the pages – this can be a good tactic to help you keep track of your thoughts. There are some blank pages at the back of the book that you can use for working out your answers, too.

Read the simple instructions on each page before tackling a puzzle. If you get stuck, read the instructions again in case there's something you missed. Work in pencil so you can rub things out and have another try.

If you are still stuck, you could also try asking an adult, although did you know that your brain is actually much more powerful than a grown-up's? When you get older, your brain gets rid of lots of bits of information it thinks it doesn't need any more. That means you might be better at solving these puzzles than older people are.

If you're **REALLY** stuck, have a peek at the answers at the back of the book, and then try to work out how you could have got to that solution yourself.

Good luck and have fun!

Let the
SCIENCE
PUZZLES
begin!

⏰ TIME ....

A habitat is another word for the environment an animal lives in.
Write the name of each animal and the habitat they belong to
beside each picture. Each habitat is used twice.

Habitats:
• woodland • ocean • mountain • rainforest

Animals:
• macaw • gorilla • dolphin • deer
• crab • pika • bighorn sheep • owl

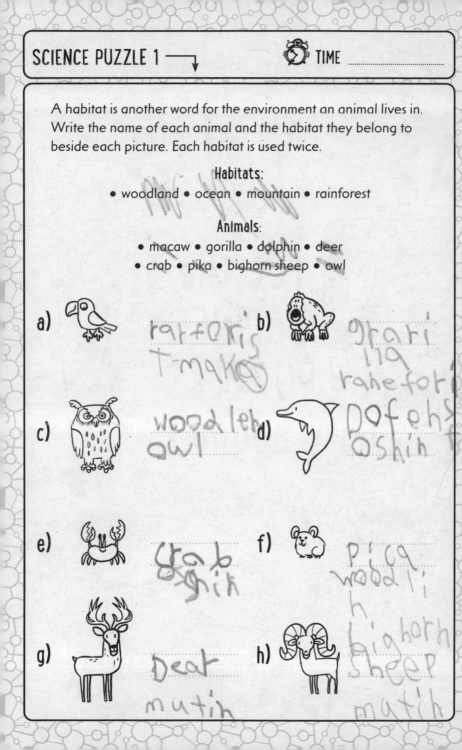

a) rarforis
tmako

b) grari
lia
rahefor

c) woodleh
owl

d) Dofehs
oshin

e) crab
shin

f) pica
woodli
h

g) Dear
mutin

h) bighorh
sheep
matih

The human body has many organs important for our survival. Can you draw a line from the body part to its function in the body?

Heart

Small intestine

Liver

Kidneys

Brain

Stomach

Lungs

Absorbs and digests most food and water

Helps the body pass waste as urine

Pumps blood through the body

Filters waste from the blood

Provides oxygen to the body

The control centre of the body

Breaks down fat and harmful chemicals

SCIENCE PUZZLE 3 ⟶

⏱ TIME ....

The woolly mammoth, a close relative of the elephant, became extinct 4,000 years ago. Can you find the woolly mammoth's exact shadow below?

Scientists often record findings from their experiments in data tables. A group of dino friends have been comparing how high they can all jump. Can you use your logic skills to fill in their results in the data table below?

- Rory is closer in age to Rocky than Raven, but Rocky is still the oldest.

- Raven can jump a quarter of her height.

- Rocky's jump falls halfway between the maximum jump and the minimum jump in the study.

Name	Age	Height (cm)	Jump (cm)
Raven	8	124	31 30
Rocky	12	137	36 35
Rory	11	132	41 40

Compare this forest scene with the one on the opposite page.

Can you spot ten differences?
Some of them have been caused
by human environmental damage.

⏰ TIME ....

When you look in a mirror you see a reflection, where the entire image is flipped around. Which image is showing the correct reflection of the scientist?

The diagram below shows the water cycle, which explains how water constantly moves on, above and below the Earth's surface. Can you spot which three tiles shown around the outside are featured in the main image?

⏰ TIME ....

There are many different layers of soil (as shown below). Can you help the dino dig down to the bedrock at the bottom?

Start

Surface

Topsoil

Subsoil

Parent rock

Bedrock

Finish

Humans have four different types of teeth. These are:

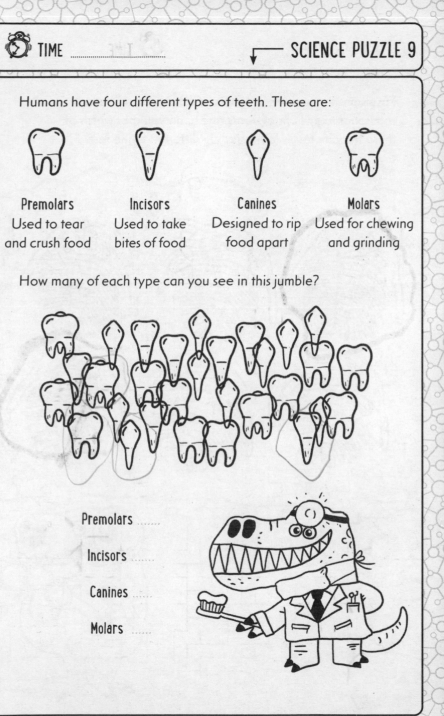

Premolars
Used to tear and crush food

Incisors
Used to take bites of food

Canines
Designed to rip food apart

Molars
Used for chewing and grinding

How many of each type can you see in this jumble?

Premolars ....

Incisors ....

Canines ......

Molars ....

Fossils are the remains or traces of plants or animals from thousands to millions of years ago. Can you spot which of these trilobite fossils looks slightly different to the rest?

Lots of dino footprints have been preserved on this piece of rock. Can you match them into pairs?

A food chain shows how different plants and animals interact with each other through the food they eat, with each one eating something else. Can you work out which living thing belongs in which of the gaps in these food chains? Each option can only be used once.

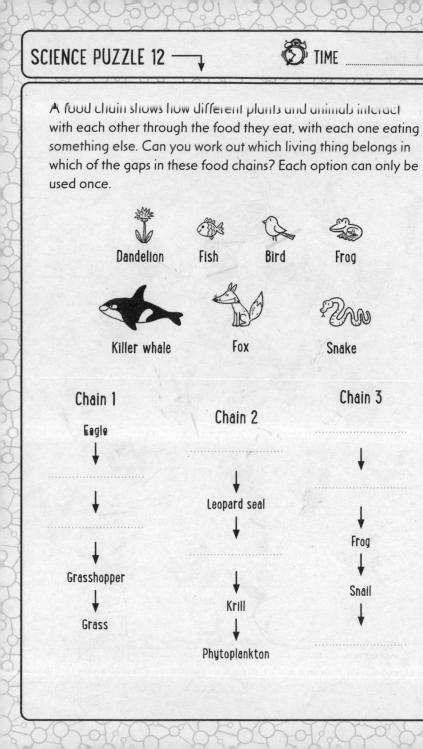

Dandelion   Fish   Bird   Frog

Killer whale   Fox   Snake

Chain 1

Eagle
↓
....
↓
....
↓
Grasshopper
↓
Grass

Chain 2

....
↓
Leopard seal
↓
....
↓
Krill
↓
Phytoplankton

Chain 3

....
↓
....
↓
Frog
↓
Snail
↓
....

Magnets are used for picking up metals that contain iron, such as steel. Which five items below can the dinosaur pick up using the magnet?

Flowers are made up of four main parts.

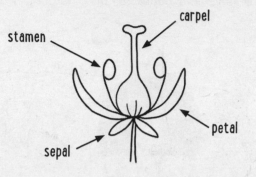

Can you draw the parts into this grid, so that only one of each is used in each row, column and bold-lined 2x2 area?

This dino is planting a Venus flytrap. Number the pictures 1–6, in the order in which they happened.

a)

b)

c)

d)

e)

f)

SCIENCE PUZZLE 16 →

Coral reefs provide nutrients to plants and animals who feed there. Can you find the following animals on the reef on the opposite page?

crab   turtle   jellyfish

starfish   reef shark

lionfish   pufferfish   barracuda

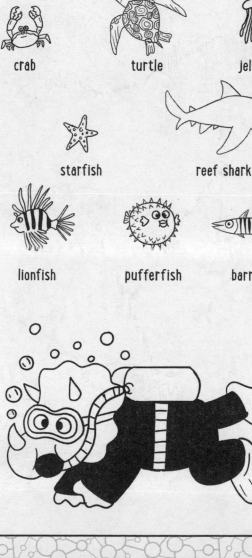

SCIENCE PUZZLE 17 →

How much do you know about the Arctic? Circle true or false for each of these statements.

a) The Arctic is located in the most southern part of the world.

True/False

b) The sea ice in the Arctic is shrinking due to climate change.

True/False

c) Polar bears and narwhals are only found in the Arctic.

True/False

d) The ice sheet at the pole in the Arctic lies over a large land mass.

True/False

e) Small shrubs and lichens grow in some parts of the Arctic.

True/False

f) The Arctic Circle includes parts of Mongolia, Greenland and Russia.

True/False

g) The Arctic is a cold, desolate region where humans have never lived.

True/False

h) During the winter, the sun is up nearly all day.

True/False

i) Polar bear populations are considered threatened due to the decrease in sea ice and food.

True/False

j) The Arctic is a large source of oil and natural gas.

True/False

Animals adapt to survive their environment. Can you guess which animal matches which facts about their adaptations?

Fennec fox   Penguin   Tiger   Armadillo

a) I have a strong sense of smell.
I have a hard shell for defence.
I have claws that I use to dig.

....

b) I can expand my throat to swallow large pieces of food.
My coat has a similar pattern to grass and tree branches.
I have soft pads on my feet.

....

c) I have a sandy coat to match my surroundings.
I have big ears, to get rid of heat.
I have thick fur for insulation on cold nights.

....

d) I huddle together with others to stay warm.
My webbed feet are great for swimming.
My bones are heavy for staying underwater.

....

These dino scientists are busy in the lab. Can you spot which one looks different to the rest?

a)

b)

c)

d)

e)

f)

SCIENCE PUZZLE 20 →

⏱ TIME ....

There are three main types of rock: igneous, sedimentary and metamorphic. Can you work out how many of each are below? Write your answers in the box when you're done.

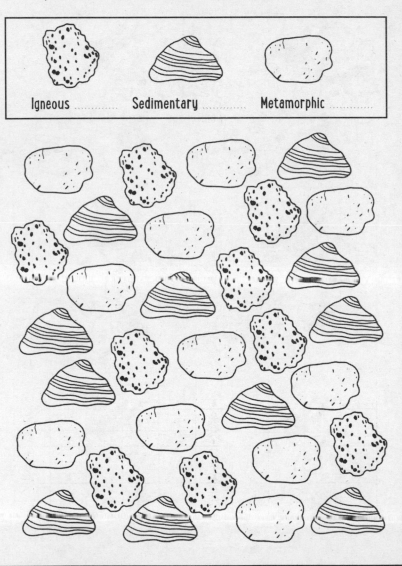

Igneous .... Sedimentary .... Metamorphic ....

Trees are either coniferous, with small, needle-like leaves, or deciduous, with wider, flat leaves. Can you guide the dino through the grid? He can only move between the trees in the order below. He can move across, up and down but not diagonally.

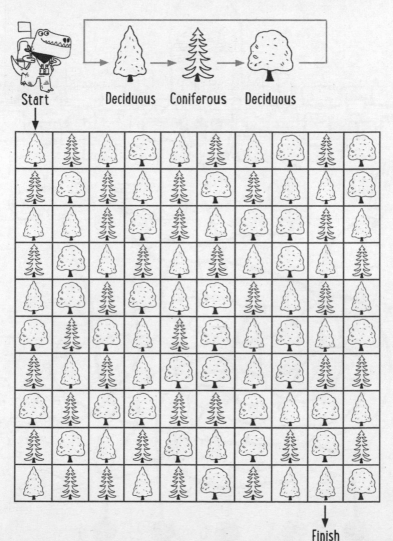

Start

Deciduous   Coniferous   Deciduous

Finish

When objects are dropped, they fall to the ground due to a force called gravity. The dinosaur has dropped some objects over a wall. Follow the lines to work out where they've landed.

Animals are put together with other animals in groups called classifications. These are based on their similar features, such as number of legs and whether they are warm- or cold-blooded. Can you draw a line from the classification to the animal? There are two animals per category.

Wolf

Bird

Bee

Amphibian

Shark

Fish

Newt

Insect

Toucan

Mammal

Manta Ray

Reptile

Frog

Snake

Butterfly

Horse

Turtle

Owl

SCIENCE PUZZLE 24 →

Our Solar System is made up of eight planets (shown below).
Fill in the blanks opposite with the name of the correct planet.

 Earth

 Jupiter

 Mars

 Mercury

 Neptune

 Saturn

 Uranus

 Venus

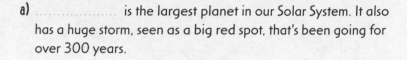

a) .... is the largest planet in our Solar System. It also has a huge storm, seen as a big red spot, that's been going for over 300 years.

b) .... is the only planet in our Solar System with standing water on its surface.

c) .... is the closest planet to the Sun and also has no wind, storms or rain.

d) .... has a gassy atmosphere of methane, making it look blue-green from far away.

e) Given the nickname, 'Red Planet', ... is full of rust-coloured dust. Scientists have sent rovers to the planet to see if it ever had life.

f) The furthest planet from the Sun, ... is blue with violent storms and freezing winds that swirl across it.

g) .... is surrounded by rings. These are made up of ice crystals and they can get as large as a house.

h) The second planet from the Sun, ... has clouds made of acid and a surface similar to molten lead.

Healthy foods, such as vegetables, give your body nutrients. Can you spot these patterns of vegetables in the grid below?

The first modern computer made its debut in 1945, and there have been lots of models developed since then. Can you match the models below with the years they were built.

• 1945   • 1964   • 1984   • 1991   • 2007

a)

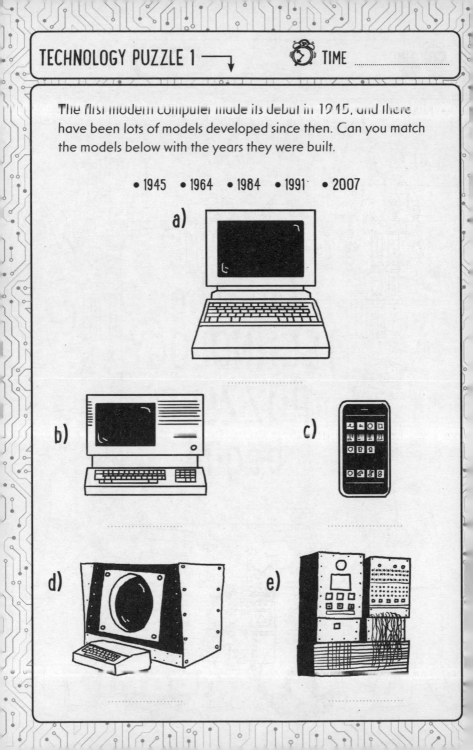

....

b)

....

c)

....

d)

....

e)

....

Humanoid robots are built with human body shapes. Can you sort these humanoid robots into identical pairs?

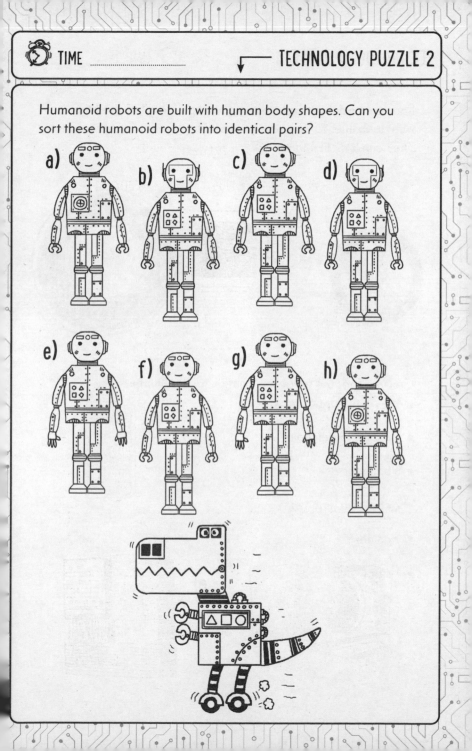

a)

b)

c)

d)

e)

f)

g)

h)

Racing wheelchairs have been developed to allow athletes with disabilities to compete at the highest level of sport. They can look like this:

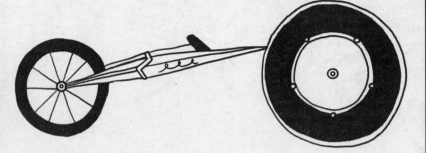

Can you spot the following items in the Paralympic race scene on the opposite page?

- 5 racing wheelchairs

- 5 balloons

- 2 cheering dino twins

- 1 camera

- 1 stopwatch

- 1 prize cup

Modern toilets use sophisticated plumbing technology to dispose of waste. Can you work out which toilet's pipe exits in which place?

Each picture below shows an individual film frame of a prehistoric megalodon leaping out of the ocean. The order of the frames has been mixed up. Can you number them from 1–9 in the order in which they happened? The first one has been done for you.

a)

....

b)

....

c)

....

d)

....

e)

....

f)

....

g)

....

h)

....

i)
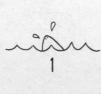
1

Facial recognition is used to identify people from videos or photos of their faces. Can you circle which dino face exactly matches the dinosaur below?

TIME ....

Electric cars are better for the environment, as they have a rechargeable battery instead of a petrol tank and an electric motor instead of an internal combustion engine (which emits fumes). Which piece, out of a) to d), can be used to complete the picture of this electric car assembly line?

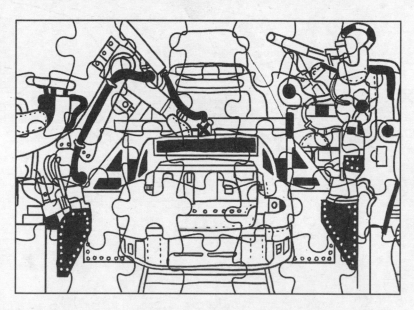

a)

b)

c)

d)

Telescopes allow us to see the stars in the night sky in more detail. Study the sky below, then look at the images in the telescopes. Only one image is showing a part of the night sky above as viewed by the dinosaurs. Which one is it?

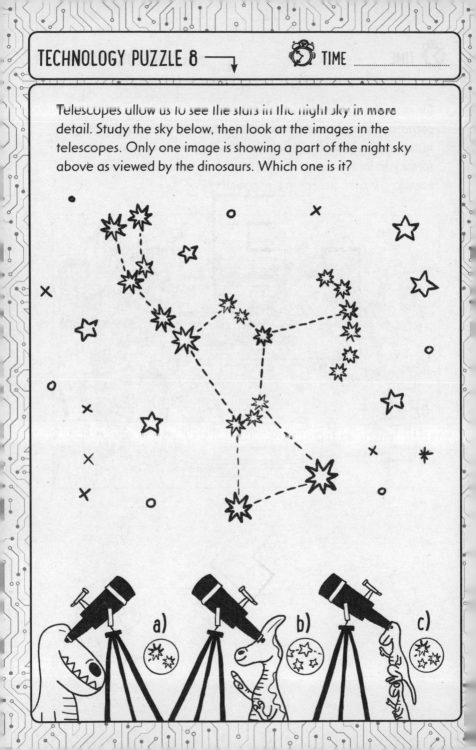

a)

b)

c)

Some of the older video games were puzzles played on a computer. One game involved rotating shapes to make them fit together like a jigsaw puzzle. Can you rotate the shapes below so they fit into the puzzle to make a complete rectangle?

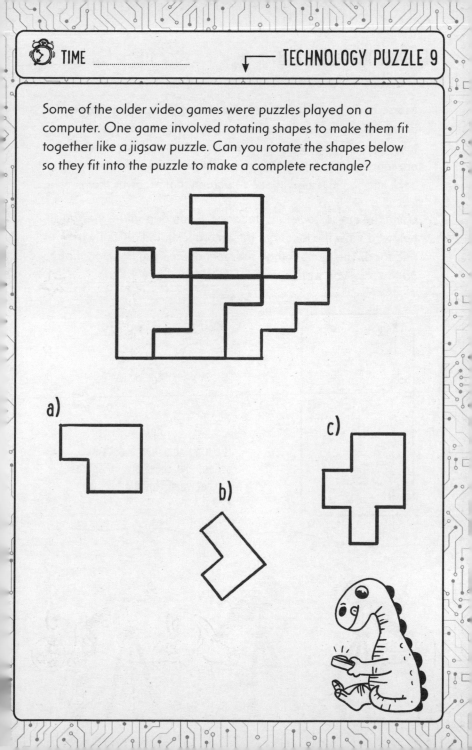

a)

b)

c)

Morse code uses dots, dashes and spaces to represent letters, punctuation and numbers. These spell out a message, and a telegraph machine converts them into electrical signals which are sent across a wire to their destination. They are converted back into the message by the telegraph that receives them.

Using the morse code key, decode the numbers in the message below to show the locations the dinosaur should NOT fly over to find food. The number that isn't mentioned is the right location to go to – can you work out what it is?

Key:
1 .----
2 ..---
3 ...--
4 ....-
5 .....
6 -....
7 --...
8 ---..
9 ----.

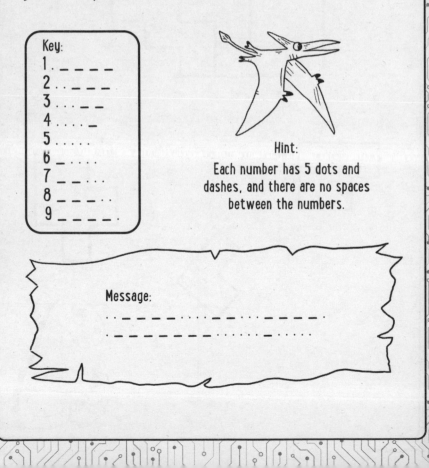

Hint:
Each number has 5 dots and dashes, and there are no spaces between the numbers.

Message:

. - - - - . . . - - . . . . . - - - - - . - - - -

. - - - - . . . . . - - - - . . . . - - - -

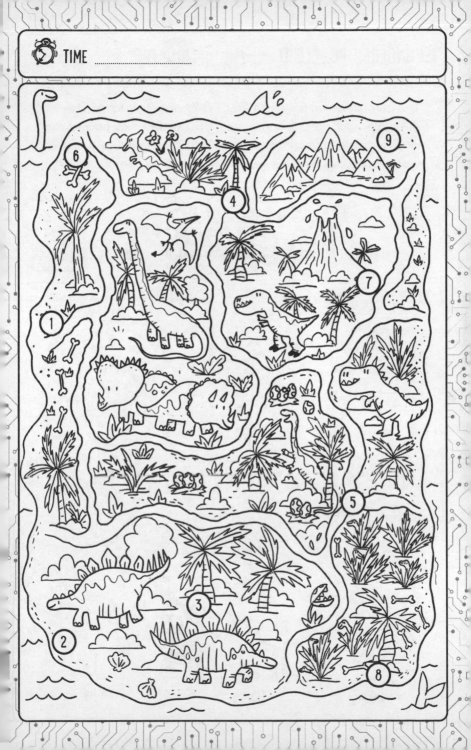

This aeroplane can only hold 20,000 kg of weight to fly. The passengers and crew only weigh 16,000 kg, but they packed too much luggage to fit on the plane. Which items can they bring with them to maximize the weight without going over the limit?

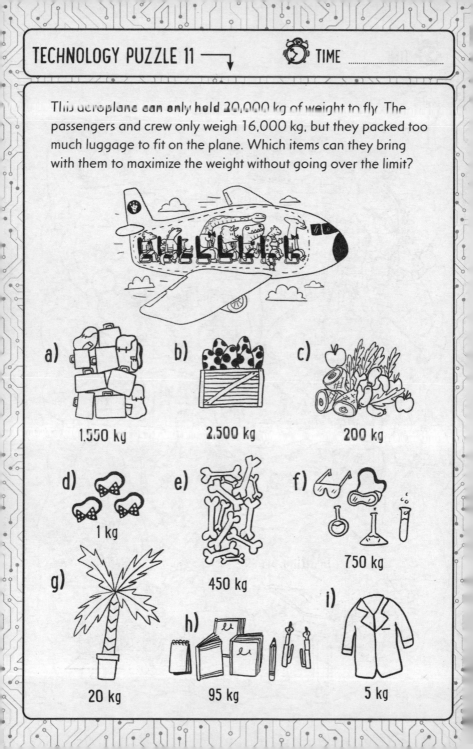

a) 1,550 kg

b) 2,500 kg

c) 200 kg

d) 1 kg

e) 450 kg

f) 750 kg

g) 20 kg

h) 95 kg

i) 5 kg

Almost everything we use to make our lives easier came from an inventor. Can you match these early inventions to their inventor?

Inventors:

Charles Babbage
Thomas Edison
Alexander Graham Bell
The Wright Brothers
Johannes Gutenberg

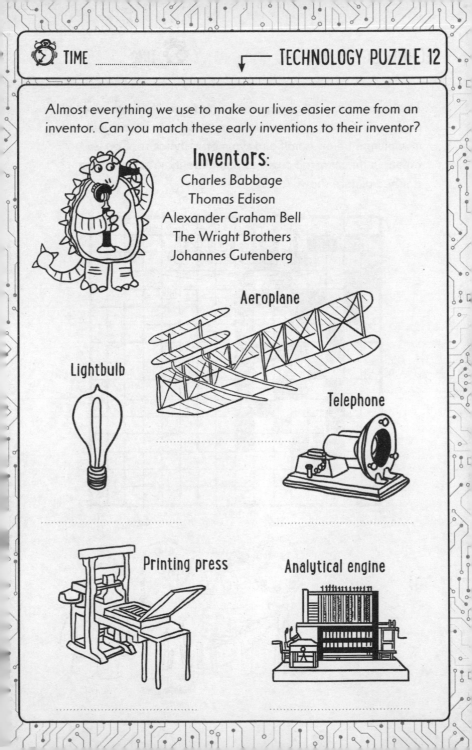

Aeroplane

Lightbulb

Telephone

Printing press

Analytical engine

Pixels are small solid squares generated on a computer display. Computers create millions of them at a time to produce images. The picture below is half of a symmetrical picture. Can you colour in the mirrored pixels to complete it? What does the finished picture show?

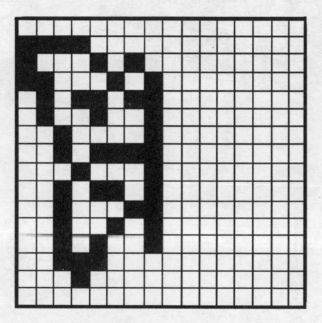

Submarines need lots of equipment to work below sea level. Only one of the four boxes below contains all of the parts and equipment from the inside of the submarine – can you find it?

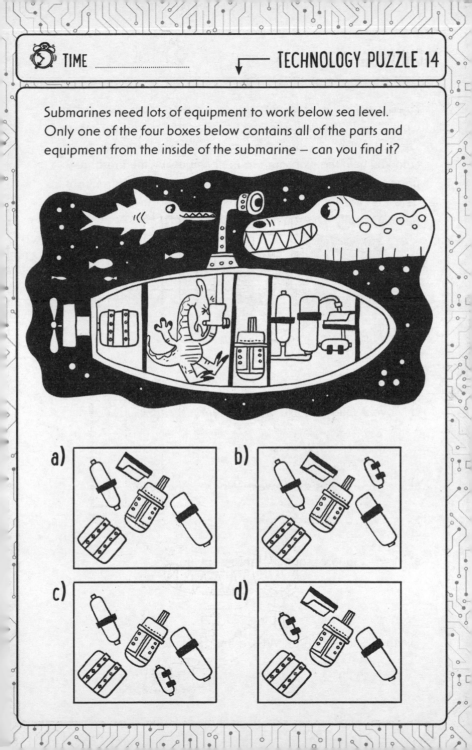

a)

b)

c)

d)

Compasses use the North Pole of the Earth to help people find what direction they need to go in.

Can you help the dinosaur use the compass on the opposite page to navigate through the fern forest? Use the instructions below to plot her coordinates. She can go up, down, left, right and diagonally. The square she starts on is D1.

a) Go 4 squares east. Where is she now?

....

b) Move 6 squares south. Where is she now?

....

c) Move 3 squares north-west. Where is she now?

....

d) Move 3 squares south-west. Where is she now?

....

e) Move 3 squares south. Where is she now?

....

f) Move 5 squares east. Where has she ended up?

....

TIME ....

Start

	A	B	C	D	E	F	G	H	I	J
1				X						
2										
3										
4										
5										
6										
7										
8										
9										
10										

Computers are told what to do using programming codes. Can you write a program using the arrow commands ↓ (go down one square), ⟵ (go left one square) and ⟶ (go right one square) to get from start to finish of the grid in exactly ten steps? Once you've written it, test it on the grid. You cannot use the squares that are blacked out. The example shows a way from start to finish in five steps.

Program example:

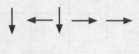

Test it:

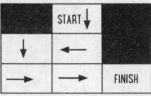

Write your program here:

....

Test it:

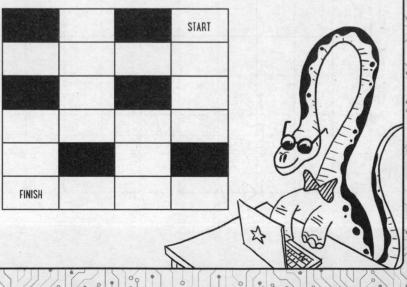

Rockets are vehicles that launch people or things into space.
This jigsaw puzzle of a rocket has some of its pieces missing.
Which four pieces should go in which slots?

a)

b)

c)

d)

e)

f)

g)

h)

⏰ TIME ....

Wind turbines create electricity as their blades rotate. It their blades are broken, they don't work. Can you guide the dinosaur through the wind farm to fix the broken turbine in the centre?

Everyone's fingerprints are different. This means that scientists can use technology to match fingerprints found at crime scenes to suspects. The three fingerprints in the box were found at a bank robbery. Can you pick them out of the fingerprint database below?

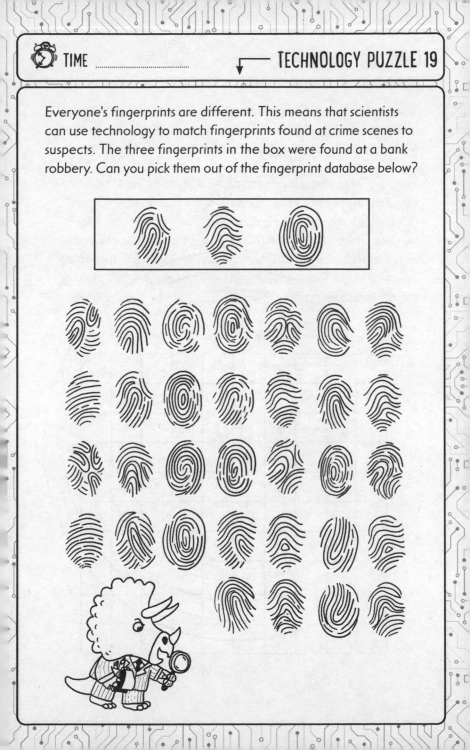

TECHNOLOGY PUZZLE 20 ⟶

Scientists use machines called seismographs to detect where in the ground earthquakes happen. Can you find where the earthquake is by reading the seismographs to the right?

The numbers are the locations of seismographs. Find them, then count the number of squares up from the location and put an 'X'. Then do the same thing down, left and to the right of the number. Once you have 4 'X's for a seismograph, connect them together with a circle. Do this for each seismograph, then draw an arrow to the space where all the circles meet – this is where the earthquake occurred.

Example:

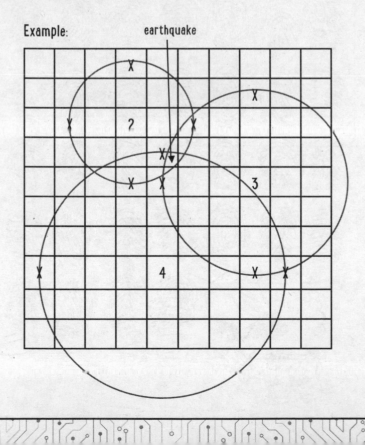

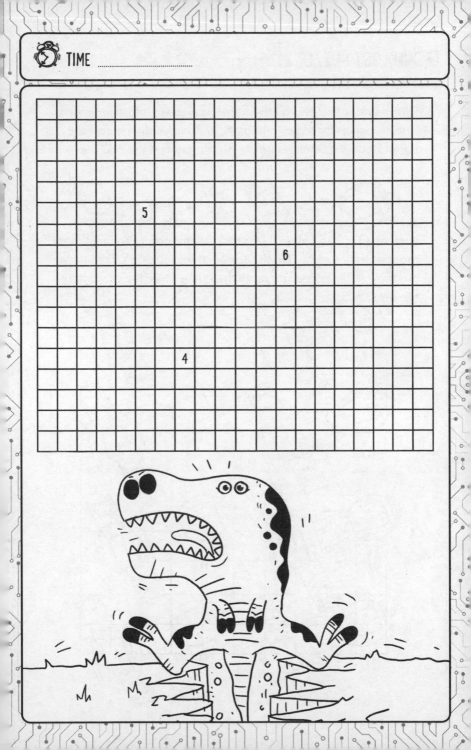

Man-made satellites orbit the Earth, collecting information and sending signals for radios and other communication across the globe. Study the satellites below – can you find the odd one out?

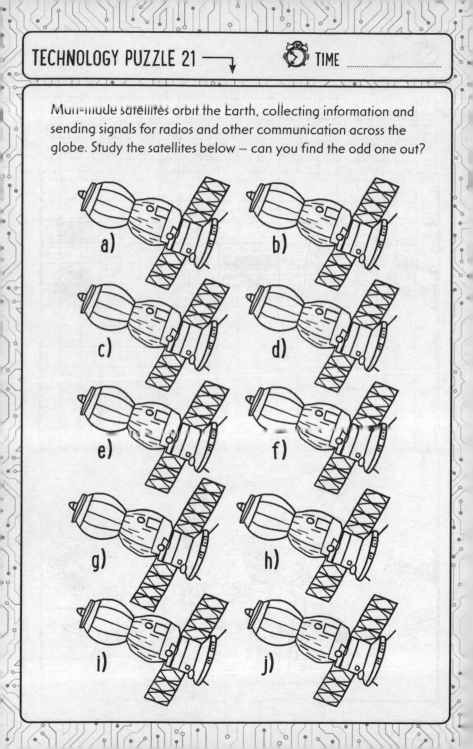

a)

b)

c)

d)

e)

f)

g)

h)

i)

j)

Kitchens are full of technology, from microwaves that heat food to washing machines that spin clothes. Can you spot ten differences between these two kitchen scenes?

Heart rate monitors are used to measure how hard your heart is working. A higher heart rate indicates more physical activity. Match what each dinosaur did today with their heart rate.

a) Jem woke up and rode her bike to school. She then cycled home after school and watched TV.

b) Monique spent most of the day in bed. She got up for dinner in the evening.

c) April is training for a big race. She went for a long run in the morning, then for a gentle swim in the afternoon.

d) Robbie slept in all morning. He then walked to a birthday party, where they played football.

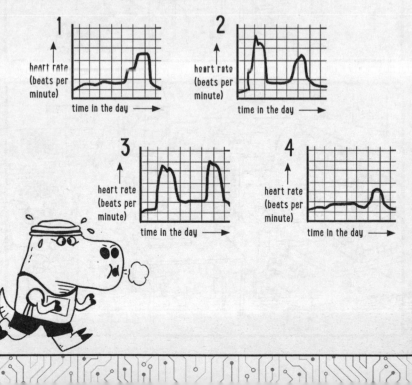

'Curiosity' is the name of a car-sized rover used to explore Mars. Match each part of the rover to its description in the list below.

Robotic arm   Used to send signals back and forth between Mars and Earth.

Laser   Measures wind speed, humidity, temperature and UV radiation.

Camera   Analyzes chemicals in rocks and soil for proof of life.

Antenna   Measures dangerous emissions coming from the Sun.

Power source   Identifies chemicals in rocks by burning holes in them.

Weather station   Identifies crystalline material in rocks and soil.

Radiation detector   Helps the whole rover operate.

Chemistry lab   Takes colour pictures and films in 3D.

Mineral detector   Used to move rocks and soil.

Electrical circuits only work when the battery (+/-) is facing the right way and the switch is closed. Can you spot the three circuits in the grid below? They are in this order:

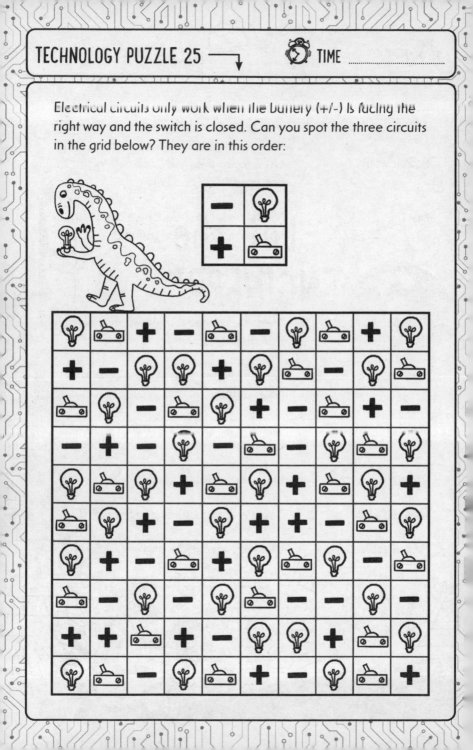

A Truss bridge uses triangles to evenly distribute the weight of the bridge, making it stable. How many triangles are formed in the gaps in the Truss bridges below? Don't count triangles that consist of more than one gap.

a)

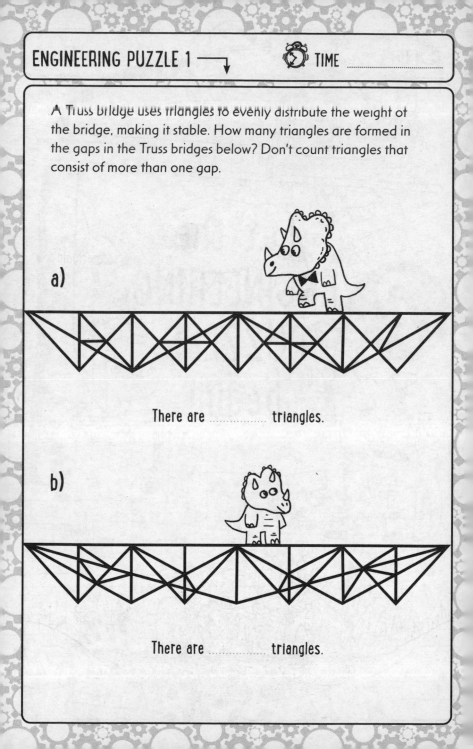

There are .... triangles.

b)

There are .... triangles.

Rain gardens are designed to catch potentially polluted rainwater from driveways, pavements and gardens. The roots of the plants, such as the marsh marigold, filter out the pollutants in the water before they can enter a stream or pond. Can you spot five marsh marigold flowers in the rain garden?

marsh marigold

Pulleys are used to help people lift things that are too heavy to lift by themselves. The more pulleys, the easier the object is for each person to lift. In each scenario on the opposite page, can you figure out how many dinosaurs are needed to pull each stone up to the top of the building site, using the pulley system?

Example question:
If each dinosaur can pull 25 kg per wheel, the pulley system has two wheels and the stone is 1,500 kg, how many dinos are needed to pull the stone?

Example answer: 30 dinosaurs
Each dino can pull 25 kg per wheel. Therefore if the pulley system has 2 wheels, each dinosaur can pull 50 kg (25 x 2). Then you need to divide the stone weight by the amount of weight each dino can pull to get the answer. So, as the stone is 1,500 kg, you would need to do 1,500 divided by 50. This equals 30 dinosaurs.

a) If each dinosaur can pull 50 kg per wheel, the pulley system has two wheels and the stone is 1,500 kg, how many dinos are needed to pull the stone?

Answer: ....

b) If each dinosaur can pull 10 kg per wheel, the pulley system has four wheels and the stone is 400 kg, how many dinos are needed to pull the stone?

Answer: ....

c) If each dinosaur can pull 100 kg per wheel, the pulley system has four wheels and the stone is 1,600 kg, how many dinos are needed to pull the stone?

Answer: ....

ENGINEERING PUZZLE 4 →

⏰ TIME ....

Some of the most common building materials are metal, wood, brick, stone, concrete and tile. Can you draw pictures of them so that they appear once in every row, column and 3x2 box?

Metal   Wood   Brick   Stone   Concrete   Tile

An oil well is a hole dug into the ground that brings oil to the surface. Look at the oil wells below. Which position does each well lead to, and which well is deep enough to reach the oil and gas layer?

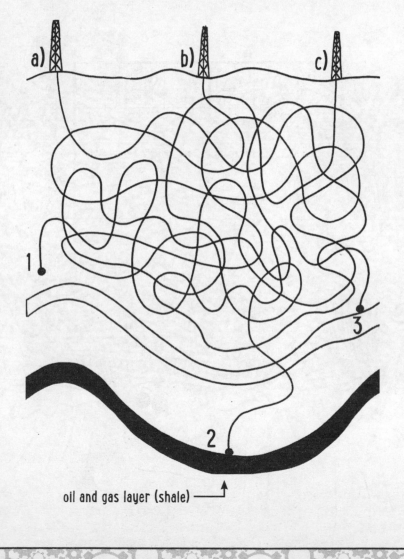

a)   b)   c)

1

3

2

oil and gas layer (shale) ⟶

Beavers are nature's engineers – they build dams out of wood and mud to slow down water and make an area where they can build their homes. Can you spot the five gaps the beaver has missed, where the water could get through?

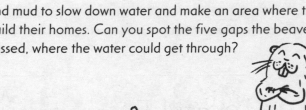

'Green bridges' are bridges of grass and trees built over roads so animals can safely cross from one habitat to another. Can you work out which pieces fit into this green bridge jigsaw puzzle?

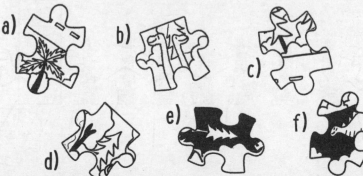

Skyscrapers are very full buildings with many, many floors. Sometimes lots of them will be built in one city, creating a whole line of skyscrapers. Study the sequences below, then draw in the empty box which building will come next in each of the skylines.

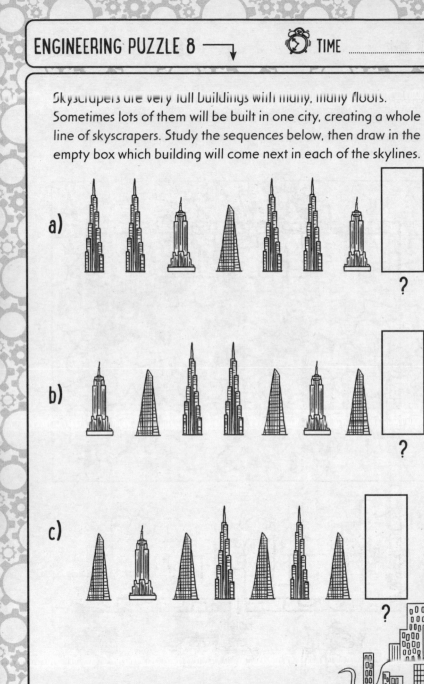

a)

b)

c)

An aqueduct is a channel used for transporting water, normally in the form of a bridge, across a gap. They were often used by the Romans. Can you find the path the water will take in this Roman-inspired maze?

Start

Finish

ENGINEERING PUZZLE 10 →

Houses need to be well-built to make sure they're safe and stable. The houses on the street opposite are looking a bit of a mess. Can you spot the following things that need fixing?

- 5 broken windows
- 4 cracked bricks
- 3 leaking pipes
- 4 cracked paving stones
- 1 collapsing roof

Drones are highly impressive pieces of engineering that fly through the air, often controlled by someone on the ground. Can you spot ten differences between these two drone scenes?

Engineers often use paper aeroplanes to test out new designs and see if they work. Can you spot the paper plane below that looks like it won't fly?

⏰ TIME ....

Ski lifts are mechanisms used to carry skiers up the mountains. The dinosaurs below have gone skiing. Can you work out which of the five shadows matches them exactly?

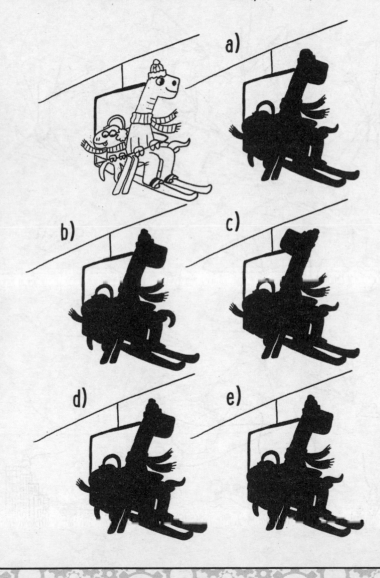

A parachute is used to slow down an object falling through the sky by increasing air resistance. Can you work out where each of these dino parachuters will land?

Cogs are wheels that have teeth around their edges. These teeth connect with the teeth on other cogs to turn each other round. Can you follow this sequence of cogs throughout the grid? You can move across, up and down but not diagonally.

Start

Finish

Bicycles have gears which can be changed to allow you to turn the pedals more easily on different road surfaces and landscapes. The dinosaur below was riding her bike to school. She started in first gear. Based on the gear changes she made, which are listed below, which gear did she end up in?

- Up two gears.

- Down one gear.

- Up three gears.

- Down one gear.

- Down one gear.

- Up three gears.

- Down two gears.

Answer: ....

Engineers have begun to develop green buildings. These have several features that reduce the amount of water and electricity consumed, and the amount of greenhouse gases sent out into the atmosphere.

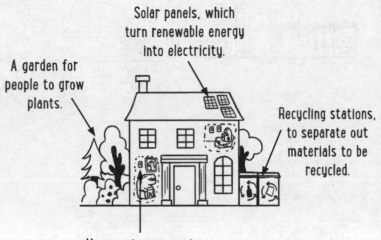

Solar panels, which turn renewable energy into electricity.

A garden for people to grow plants.

Recycling stations, to separate out materials to be recycled.

Movement sensors, to turn off the lights when people aren't around.

Spike lives in the green dinosaur village shown on the opposite page. Using the clues below, can you work out where he lives?

- Spike's house doesn't have a garden.

- It does have movement detectors.

- It has three or more solar panels.

- It has recycling stations.

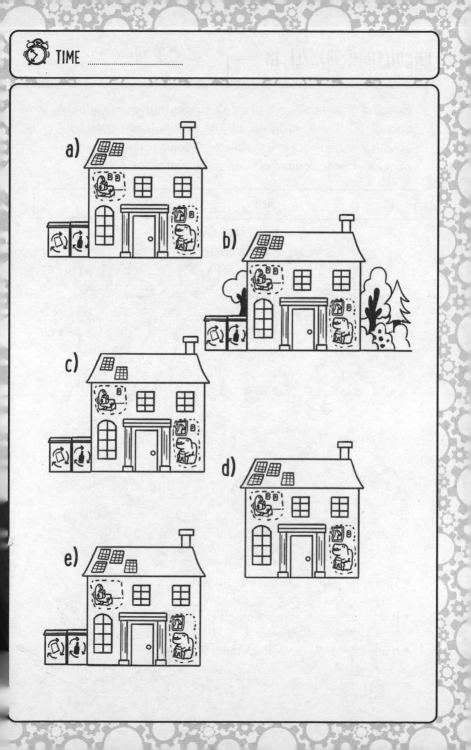

Conductors are objects that an electric current can flow freely through. They are mostly metal. The materials that make up conductors are important in electrical engineering. How many of each of these conductors can you count below?

Bell	Key	Coin ....

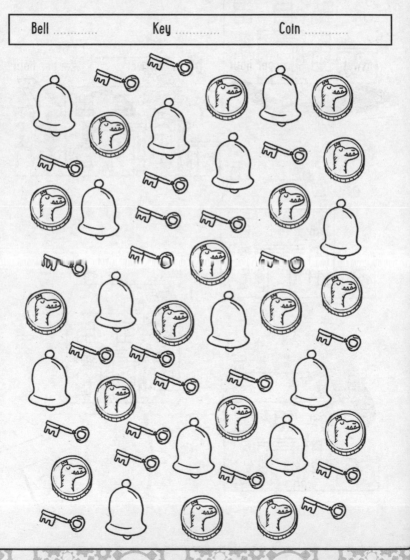

The average jet plane needs to reach a speed of 280 km per hour to take off. Solve the sums next to each of these planes in order to work out which one is going fast enough to do this.

a) 50 x 10
   – 40
   ÷ 2

Answer .... km per hour

b) 60 + 30
   x 3
   + 8

Answer .... km per hour

c) 100 ÷ 5
   + 10
   x 8

Answer .... km per hour

d) 80 – 5
   x 2
   + 125

Answer .... km per hour

e) 25 x 4
   + 200
   – 10

Answer .... km per hour

Shipping containers are designed to safely transport materials on ships. The sets below each contain a certain number of shipping containers. These need to be loaded on to the three ships below, which can only carry a certain number of containers each. Which sets should be loaded on to which ships so that all the cargo can be carried without going over the cargo limits?

Set 1

55 containers

Set 2

37 containers

Set 3

22 containers

Set 4

39 containers

Set 5

42 containers

Set 6

58 containers

Set 7

41 containers

Ship a) can hold up to 200 containers

Ship b) can hold up to 60 containers

Ship c) can hold up to 40 containers

Engineers are constantly looking for ways to reuse rubbish and reduce waste to help the planet. Can you find ten plastic bottles that have been changed into vases and plant pots in time for the dinosaur ball? Hint: they all contain flowers.

Engineers design medical equipment that help people who are ill or injured, such as X-ray machines. Study the dinosaur, then compare it to the X-rays. Can you find the matching one?

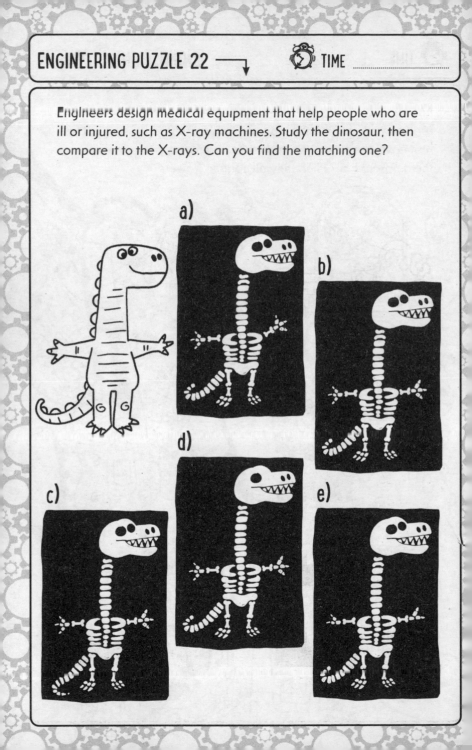

a)

b)

c)

d)

e)

Keys and locks are part of mechanical engineering. Keys have to slot perfectly into locks in order for them to open. Look at the locks below. Which one will the dinosaur's key fit in to?

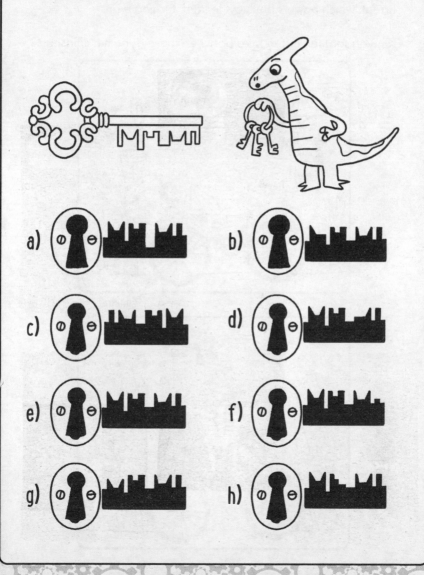

Dynamos are machines that turn movement into electricity. These dynamos can be attached to the wheels of bicycles, so that as the wheel goes round it turns the dynamo. This produces an electrical current, which powers the bicycle light, turning it on.

Can you spot ten differences between these dynamic dinosaurs?

dynamo

Dynamos only work when turning, so if the bicycle stops moving, the light will go out. These four dinosaurs are on their way home — can you follow the white paths inside the maze to work out which one will be able to make it back to the house with their light on the whole way? Remember, they can't stop!

ENGINEERING PUZZLE 26 →

⏱ TIME ....

Did you know that rollercoaster cars don't have engines? They are designed to work without them, using gravity instead. Looking at the puzzle below, can you work out which dinosaur is riding which themed rollercoaster ride?

a)

b)

c)

1

2

3

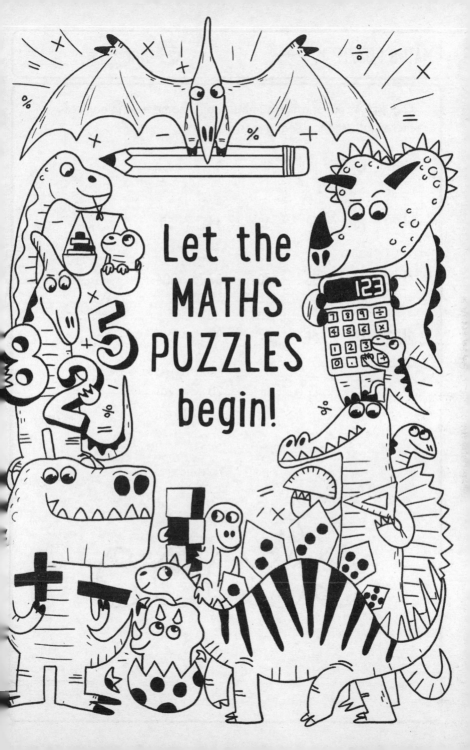

Can you work out which number should come next in each of these mathematical sequences?

a) 17   15   13   11   9   7   ....

b) 20   26   32   38   44   50   ....

c) 19   36   53   70   87   104   ....

d) 729   243   81   27   9   3   ....

e) 10   11   13   16   20   25   ....

These young dinos — Albie, Bernie and Chloe — all share the same birthday. On their most recent birthday, Bernie noticed that:

- One year ago, Chloe was half the age that Albie is now.

- The difference between Albie and Bernie's ages is the same as the difference between Bernie's and Chloe's ages.

- In two years time, Bernie will be the same age that Albie is now.

- Albie is four years older than Chloe.

- The total of all three of their ages is 24.

How old are they?

Albie is ....   Bernie is ....   Chloe is ....

Take a look at this picture, which consists of lots of overlapping circles. How many circles can you count in total?

Answer: ....

To solve these diagonal sum sudoku puzzles, place numbers from 1 to 4 once each into every row, column and bold-lined 2x2 box. Each of the numbers outside the grid reveals the sum of the diagonal pointed to by its arrow.

Here's a finished example:

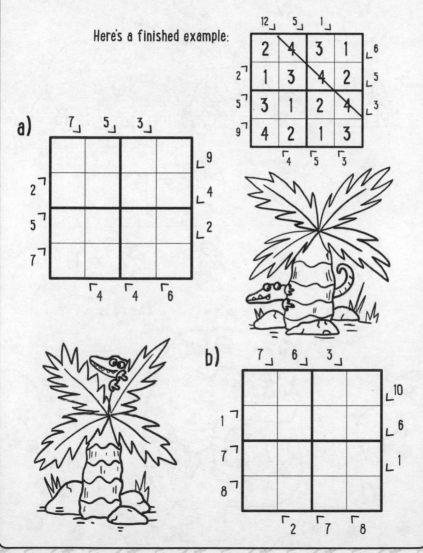

a)

b)

TIME ....

Each of there types of fruit represents a different number. Can you work out these numbers, and write them in the gaps at the bottom of the page?

 = 11

 = 13

 = 14

 = 19

Apple is .... Banana is .... Cherry is ....

Can you work out what happens to each number as it passes through the centre box in each drawing? A mathematical operation is taking place, such as adding, subtracting or multiplying. For example, in the first puzzle what would you need to do to change 2 to 13, change 7 to 18 and so on?

a)

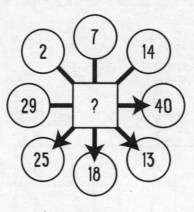

Answer: ....

b)

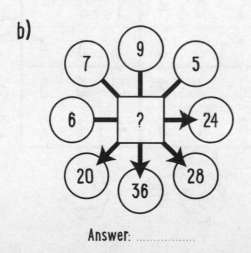

Answer: ....

To solve these sudoku X/V puzzles, place numbers into the empty squares so that 1 to 6 appear once each in every row, column and bold-lined 3x2 box.

Wherever an 'X' joins two squares then the sum of those two squares is 10. Wherever a 'V' joins two squares then the sum of those two squares is 5. This is because X=10 and V=5 in Roman numerals.

Here's a finished example:

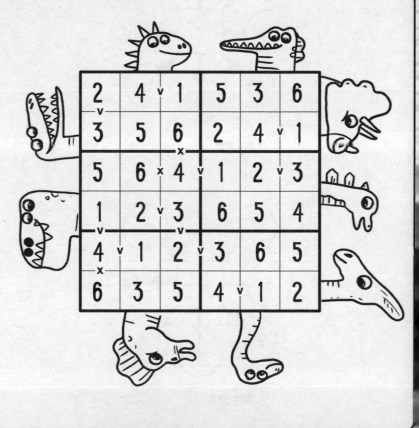

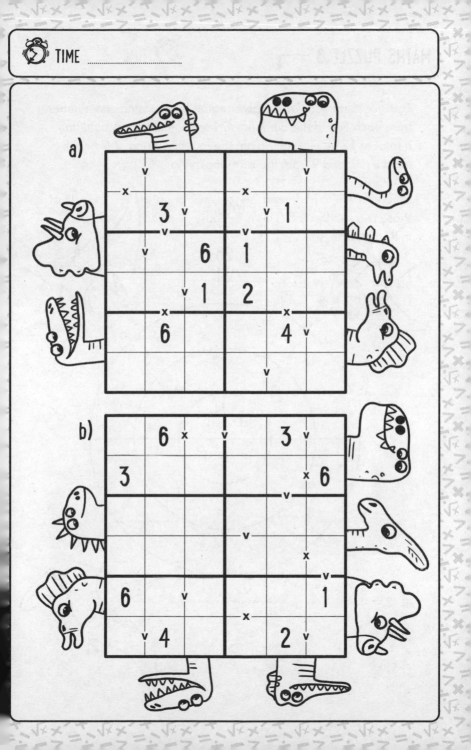

MATHS PUZZLE 8 →

⏰ TIME ....

Can you form each of the given totals by choosing one number from each ring of this dartboard? For example, you could get a total of 12 by picking 1 from the innermost ring, 2 from the middle ring and 9 from the outermost ring.

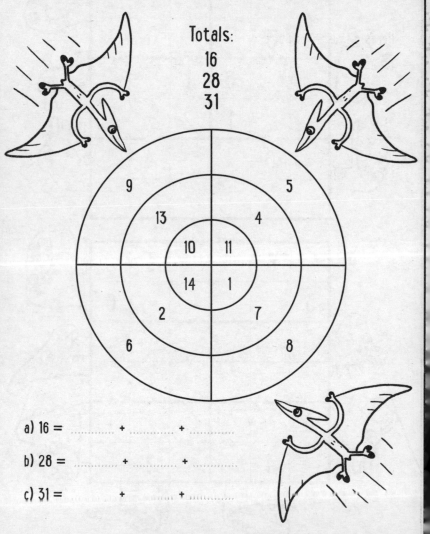

Totals:
16
28
31

a) 16 = ... + ... + ...

b) 28 = ... + ... + ...

c) 31 = ... + ... + ...

In each of the puzzles below, start with the number on the left and then perform each of the calculations shown in order. What number do you end up with?

Here's a finished example:

12   +10   –14   x5   = 40

a) 19   +19   –10   ÷4   = ...

b) 90   ÷10   x5   –20   = ...

c) 150   –90   ÷12   x6   = ...

Can you cross out one number on each of the rows below, so that what remains forms a mathematical sequence?

Here's a finished example:

2   4   6   ~~7~~   8   10   12

Sequence: add 2 at each step

a) 5   6   7   9   11   13   15

Sequence:...

b) 87   84   81   79   78   75   72

Sequence:...

c) 101   90   80   79   68   57   46

Sequence:...

d) 1   2   4   8   12   16   32

Sequence:...

⌐ MATHS PUZZLE 11

To solve these frame sudoku puzzles, place a number from 1 to 4 into every empty square so that they appear once each in every row, column and bold-lined 2x2 box. The numbers outside the grid reveal the sum of the two nearest numbers in the corresponding row or column.

Here's a finished example:

	4	6	4	6	
5	3	2	1	4	5
5	1	4	3	2	5
5	4	1	2	3	5
5	2	3	4	1	5
	6	4	6	4	

a)

	5	5	5	5	
6	2			3	4
4					6
6					4
4	1			4	6
	5	5	5	5	

b)

	5	5	3	7	
4					6
6			1		4
6		4			4
4					6
	5	5	7	3	

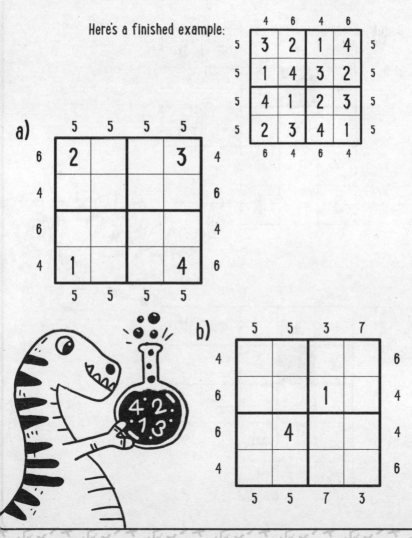

Place a number from 1 to 9 into each empty white square, so all four sums in each puzzle are correct. You can't use any number more than once — not even across the two puzzles. This means that one of the numbers from 1 to 9 won't be used, but all the rest will be used once each.

a)

	+		=	6
+	■	÷		
	x		=	3
=		=		
5		4		

b)

	+		=	16
x	■	-		
	-		=	2
=		=		
72		1		

Which of the three shapes — the circle, square or triangle — weighs the most? And which of the three shapes weighs the least?

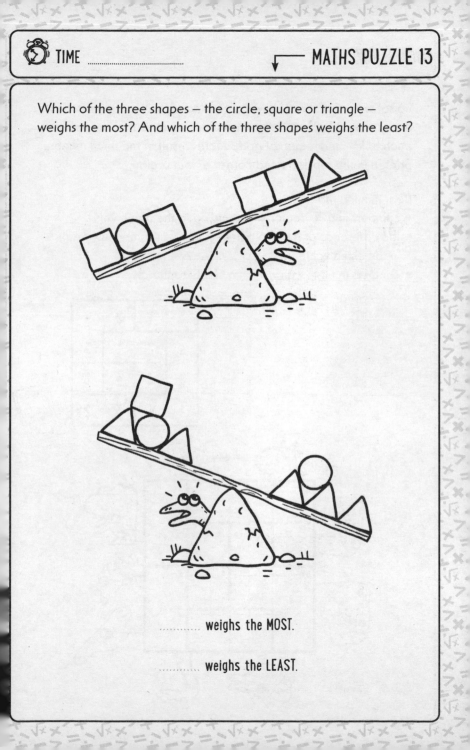

.... weighs the MOST.

.... weighs the LEAST.

To solve these Calcudoku puzzles, place 1 to 4 once each into every row and column. You must place them so that the values in each bold-lined region of grid squares result in the small number printed in the top-left hand corner of that region.

Bear in mind that:
- numbers in a "+" region must add up to the given value
- the difference of the two numbers in a "-" region must result in the given value
- numbers in a "x" region must multiply to the given value

Here's a finished example:

4+ 3	1	10+ 2	4
32× 4	2× 2	1	3
2	12× 3	4	1
1	4	1- 3	2

a)

b)

10 +		7 +	
			3
1	48 ×		
12 ×			

c)

3 +	3 −	1 −	
		12 ×	
7 +		1 −	4 ×
1 −			

In the distant land of Dinotopia they have five different values of coin, as shown below.

Assuming that you have as many of each value of coin as you might need, can you answer the following questions?

a) What is the minimum number of coins you need in order to have a total of exactly 75d?

Answer: ....

b) If you use no more than two of any value of coin, what is the maximum number of coins you can use to spend exactly 75d?

Answer: ....

c) How many different combinations of coins are possible in order to make up a total of 8d? For example, you could use 5d + 2d + 1d.

Answer: ....

Which balloons would you pick in order to form each of the totals below? The numbers on the balloons must add up to the total, and you can use each number only once per total. For example, you could form 14 by picking the 4 and 10 balloons.

a) Total: 18

Answer: ....

b) Total: 29

Answer: ....

c) Total: 34

Answer: ....

d) Total: 42

Answer: ....

Place a number from 1 to 4 into each square so that no number repeats in any row or column. Numbers must follow the 'greater than' signs, which are arrows that always point from the bigger number to the smaller number of a pair of squares.

For example, you could have '2 > 1' since 2 is greater than 1, but '1 > 2' would be wrong because 1 is not greater in value than 2.

Here's a finished example:

4	2 < 3	1
2	4	1	3
1	3 < 4	2
3	1 < 2	4

a)

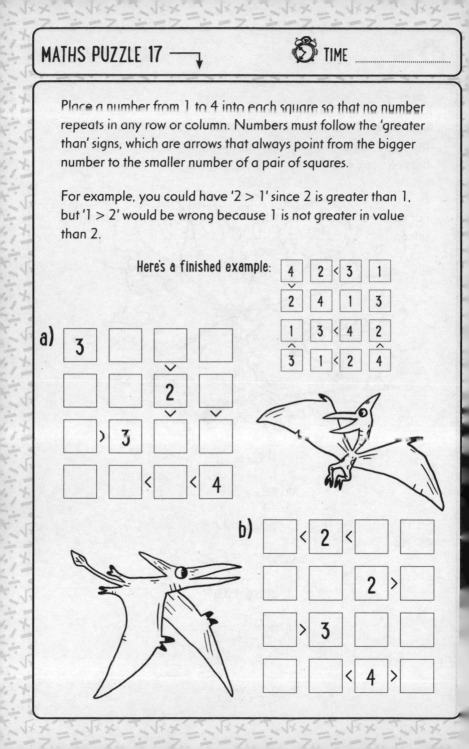

b)

Can you use each of these mathematical operations to join a pair of numbers? Each number, and each operation, should be used only once. There are multiple ways of joining some pairs, but only one way of doing so which allows all of the numbers and operations to be used once each.

For example, you could use the '×5' operation to join 2 and 10, since 2 × 5 = 10.

Numbers:

15		10		20
45	18		35	38
2		8		7

Operations:

+20   ×2   ×3

×5   ÷4

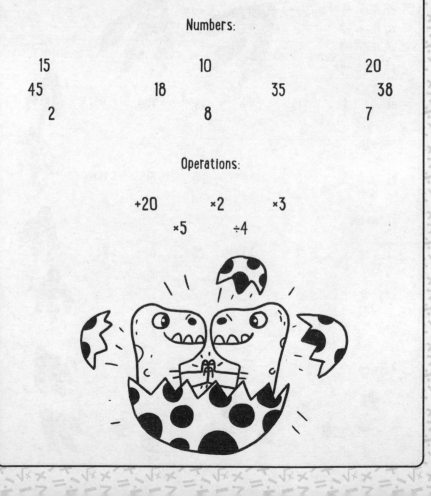

There are four different number sequences given below, and four different sets of instructions. Can you work out which instruction is being used to create each sequence? Each instruction is used by only one sequence.

Bear in mind that you don't need to do the full set of calculations for each sequence to work out which instruction is being used for it.

Instructions
x2 then −1
x3 then −2
x4 then −3
x5 then −10

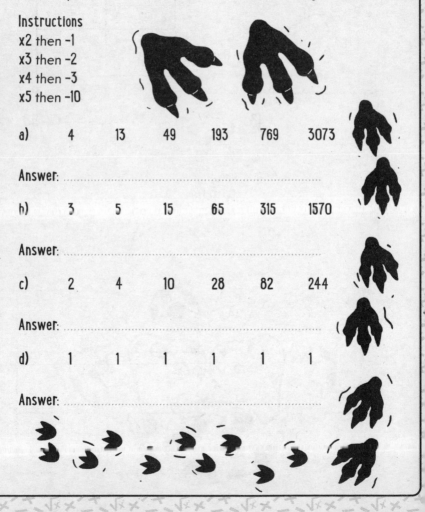

a)   4   13   49   193   769   3073

Answer: ....

b)   3   5   15   65   315   1570

Answer: ....

c)   2   4   10   28   82   244

Answer: ....

d)   1   1   1   1   1   1

Answer: ....

To solve these arrow sudokus, place numbers from 1 to 6 so that they appear once each in every row, column and bold-lined 3x2 box. Also, each circled number must be equal to the total of the numbers along its attached arrow.

Here's a finished example:

6	1	3	5	2	4
4	2	5	6	1	3
1	5	4	3	6	2
3	6	2	1	4	5
2	3	6	4	5	1
5	4	1	2	3	6

a)

				2	5
3			6	4	1
				3	
	2				
2	6	4			3
5	3				

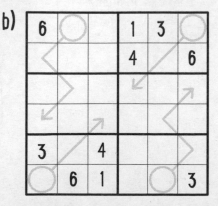

b)

6			1	3	
			4		6
3		4			
	6	1			3

See if you can answer these time-based questions:

a) If it's 5:30pm now, how many minutes will have passed by the time it's 7:45pm today?

Answer: ....

b) I go to bed at 9:30pm, and finished my dinner 3 hours earlier. Dinner took half an hour to eat, and then before that I was at home for 2 hours after being at school all day. Given that school lasted 7 hours, at what time did I start school?

Answer: ....

c) If the day three days before the day after tomorrow is Thursday, then what day is it today?

Answer: ....

d) Which of these three numbers is the smallest: 1) the number of days in a week; 2) the number of months in a year with fewer than 31 days; 3) the number of months in a year with a letter 'r' in them?

Answer: ....

TIME ....

MATHS PUZZLE 22

How many rectangles can you count in this image? Include every one you can find, including the large one all around the edge of the image and ones that overlap each other.

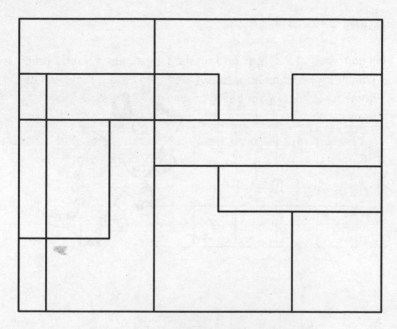

Answer: ....

MATHS PUZZLE 23 →

Write a number into each empty pyramid block, so that each block contains a number equal to the sum of the two numbers directly beneath it.

Here's a finished example:

a)

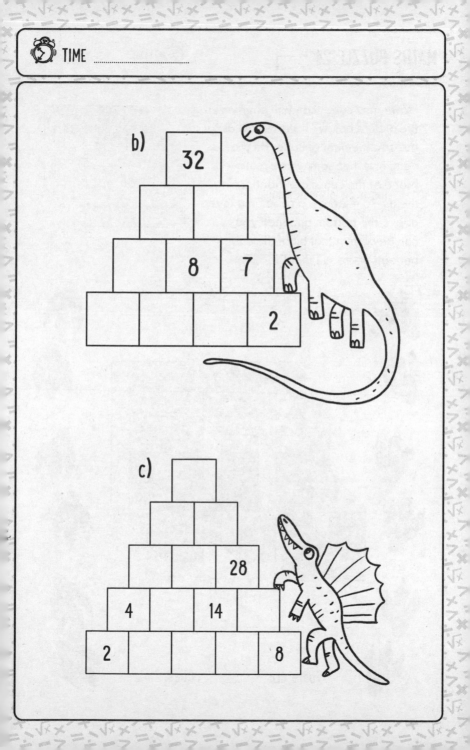

b)

32

| 8 | 7 |

| 2 |

c)

| 28 |

| 4 | 14 |

| 2 | 8 |

TIME ....

How many cubes can you count in the picture below? It started off as the arrangement of cubes on the right, and then some were removed. None of the cubes are 'floating' in the air, so if there is a cube on a layer above the bottom one then you can be certain that all of the cubes beneath it are still there too.

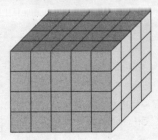

There are .... cubes.

Can you help the dino back to his friends, by finding a route from the entrance at the top of the maze to the exit at the bottom?

Once you've solved it, add up the values that you must travel over on the route from the entrance to the exit, ignoring any dead ends you previously travelled along. What is the total of all of those values?

Answer: ....

To solve this integer multiple sudoku puzzle, place numbers from 1 to 6 once each into every row, column and bold-lined 3x2 box.

Every place where two touching squares contain values where one is an integer (whole number) multiple of the other is marked with a circle between the two squares. The circle tells you how many times larger one number is than the other, so for example if it contains a '3' then you know that one number is three times as large as the other.

Here's a finished example:

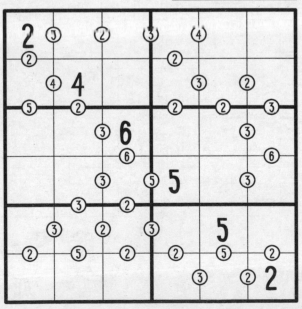

All of the ANSWERS

SCIENCE PUZZLE 1

a) Macaw
   Rainforest

b) Gorilla
   Rainforest

c) Owl
   Woodland

d) Dolphin
   Ocean

e) Crab
   Ocean

f) Pika
   Moutain

g) Deer
   Woodland

h) Bighorn sheep
   Moutain

SCIENCE PUZZLE 2

Lungs: provides oxygen to the body
Heart: pumps blood through the body
Small intestine: absorbs and digests most food and water
Liver: filters waste from the blood
Kidneys: helps the body pass waste as urine
Brain: the control centre of the body
Stomach: breaks down fat and harmful chemicals

SCIENCE PUZZLE 3

d) is showing the exact shadow.

SCIENCE PUZZLE 4

Raven is 124 cm tall.
Rocky jumped 36 cm.
Rory is 11 years old.

SCIENCE PUZZLE 5

SCIENCE PUZZLE 6

c) is showing the correct reflection.

SCIENCE PUZZLE 7

d), g) and i) are featured in the main image.

SCIENCE PUZZLE 8

SCIENCE PUZZLE 9

Premolars: 9
Incisors: 7
Canines: 10
Molars: 4

SCIENCE PUZZLE 10

e) is slightly different to the rest.

SCIENCE PUZZLE 11

SCIENCE PUZZLE 12

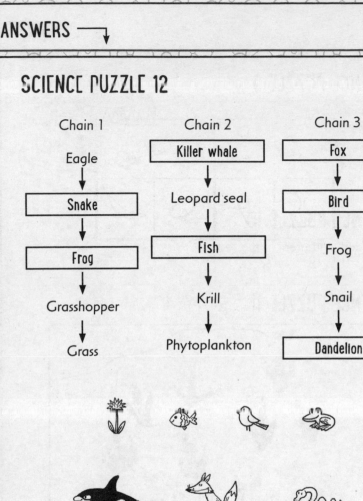

Chain 1

Eagle
↓
Snake
↓
Frog
↓
Grasshopper
↓
Grass

Chain 2

Killer whale
↓
Leopard seal
↓
Fish
↓
Krill
↓
Phytoplankton

Chain 3

Fox
↓
Bird
↓
Frog
↓
Snail
↓
Dandelion

SCIENCE PUZZLE 13

The dinosaur can pick up the **key**, the **hammer**, the **frying pan**, the **scissors** and the **cheese grater**.

SCIENCE PUZZLE 14

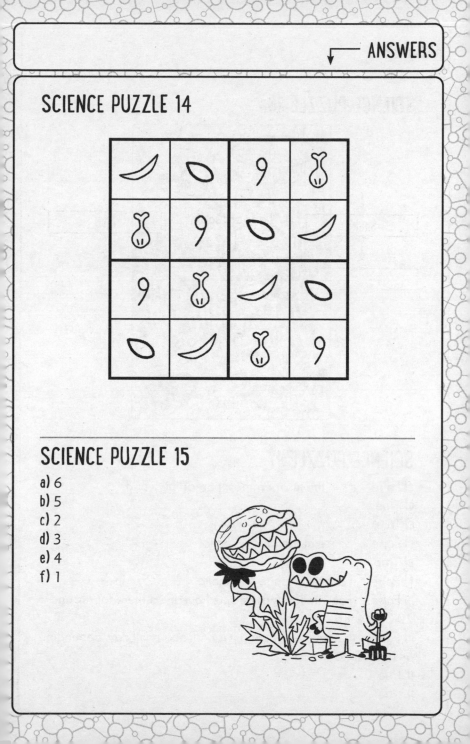

SCIENCE PUZZLE 15

a) 6
b) 5
c) 2
d) 3
e) 4
f) 1

SCIENCE PUZZLE 16

SCIENCE PUZZLE 17

a) False – it's in the northernmost part of the world.

b) True

c) True

d) False – the ice at the pole is sea ice.

e) True

f) False – it doesn't include Mongolia.

g) False – many Indigenous people have lived there for around 20,000 years.

h) False – the sun is down, and it is dark nearly all day, depending on how far north you are.

i) True

j) True

SCIENCE PUZZLE 18

a) Armadillo
b) Tiger
c) Fennec fox
d) Penguin

SCIENCE PUZZLE 19

a) looks different from the rest.

SCIENCE PUZZLE 20

Igenous: 9
Sedimentary: 11
Metamorphic: 11

SCIENCE PUZZLE 21

SCIENCE PUZZLE 22

a) 3
b) 4
c) 5
d) 1
e) 2

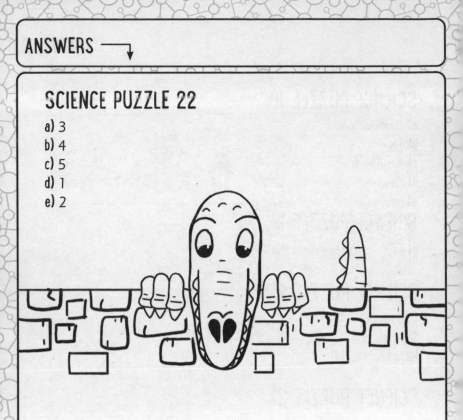

SCIENCE PUZZLE 23

Bird: toucan and owl
Amphibian: frog and newt
Fish: shark and manta ray
Insect: bee and butterfly
Mammal: wolf and horse
Reptile: snake and turtle

SCIENCE PUZZLE 24

a) Jupiter
b) Earth
c) Mercury
d) Uranus
e) Mars
f) Neptune
g) Saturn
h) Venus

SCIENCE PUZZLE 25

TECHNOLOGY PUZZLE 1

a) 1991
b) 1984
c) 2007
d) 1964
e) 1945

TECHNOLOGY PUZZLE 2

The pairs are:
a) and h)
b) and d)
c) and f)
e) and g)

TECHNOLOGY PUZZLE 3

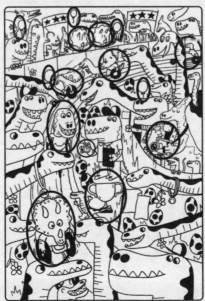

TECHNOLOGY PUZZLE 4

a) 2
b) 1
c) 3

TECHNOLOGY PUZZLE 5

a) 9
b) 4
c) 6
d) 2
e) 8
f) 3
g) 5
h) 7
i) 1

TECHNOLOGY PUZZLE 6

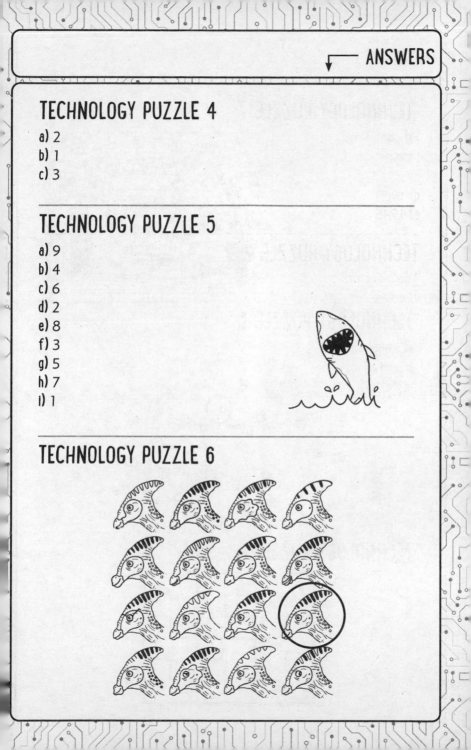

TECHNOLOGY PUZZLE 7

b) completes
the picture.

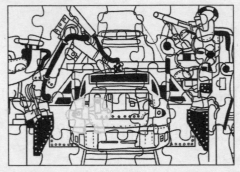

TECHNOLOGY PUZZLE 8

a) is showing
a part of the
night sky.

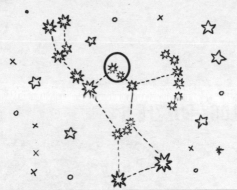

TECHNOLOGY PUZZLE 9

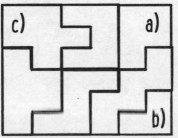

TECHNOLOGY PUZZLE 10

The Morse code message is: **26791845**. Therefore the dinosaur should fly over location **3**.

TECHNOLOGY PUZZLE 11

They can bring items b), c), e), f), h) and i).

TECHNOLOGY PUZZLE 12

Aeroplane: The Wright Brothers
Lightbulb: Thomas Edison
Telephone: Alexander Graham Bell
Printing press: Johannes Gutenberg
Analytical engine: Charles Babbage

TECHNOLOGY PUZZLE 13

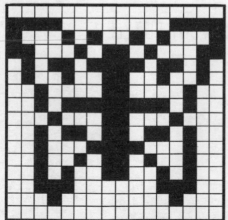

The picture is a butterfly.

TECHNOLOGY PUZZLE 14

b) contains all the parts and equipment from inside the submarine.

TECHNOLOGY PUZZLE 15

a) H1
b) H7
c) E4
d) B7
e) B10
f) G10

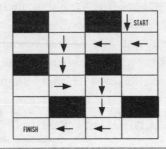

TECHNOLOGY PUZZLE 16

The program written out was:

↓ ← ← ↓ ↓ → ↓ ↓ ← ←

TECHNOLOGY PUZZLE 17

TECHNOLOGY PUZZLE 18

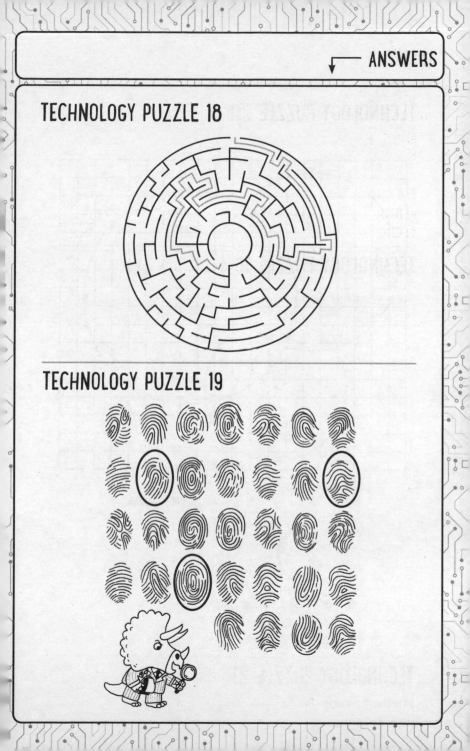

TECHNOLOGY PUZZLE 19

TECHNOLOGY PUZZLE 20

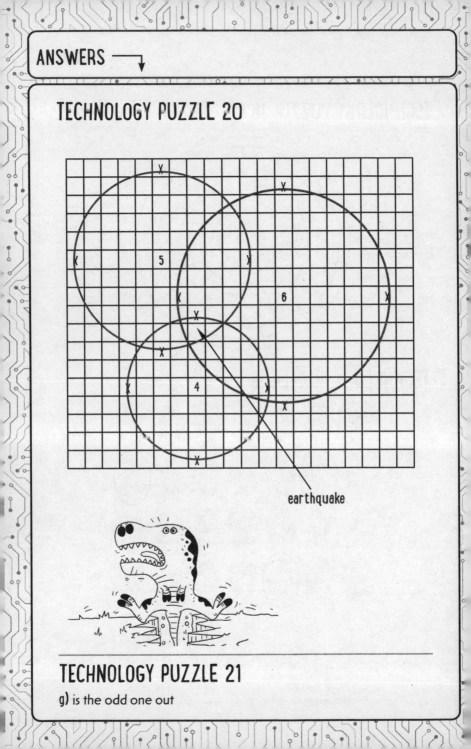

earthquake

TECHNOLOGY PUZZLE 21

g) is the odd one out

TECHNOLOGY PUZZLE 22

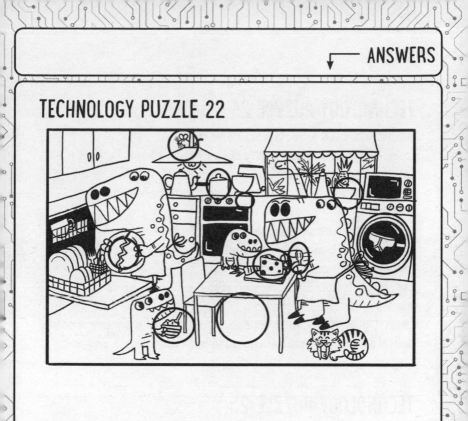

TECHNOLOGY PUZZLE 23

a) 3 (as the heart-rate movements for cycling are of similar size)
b) 4 (as there was very little activity all day)
c) 2 (as the run would have raised her heart rate more than the swim)
d) 1 (as there was little activity until later in the day)

TECHNOLOGY PUZZLE 21

Robotic arm: used to move rocks and soil.

Laser: identifies chemicals in rocks by burning holes in them.

Camera: takes colour pictures and films in 3D.

Antenna: used to send signals back and forth between Mars and Earth.

Power source: helps the whole rover operate.

Weather station: measures wind speed, humidity, temperature and UV radiation.

Radiation detector: measures dangerous emissions coming from the Sun.

Chemistry lab: analyzes chemicals in rocks and soil for proof of life.

Mineral detector: identifies crystalline material in rocks and soil.

TECHNOLOGY PUZZLE 25

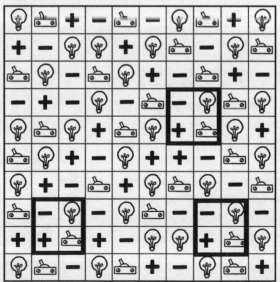

ENGINEERING PUZZLE 1

a) 38 triangles
b) 44 triangles

ENGINEERING PUZZLE 2

ENGINEERING PUZZLE 3

a) 15 dinosaurs
b) 10 dinosaurs
c) 4 dinosaurs

ANSWERS

ENGINEERING PUZZLE 1

ENGINEERING PUZZLE 5

a) 1
b) 2
c) 3

b) is deep enough to reach the oil and gas layer.

ENGINEERING PUZZLE 6

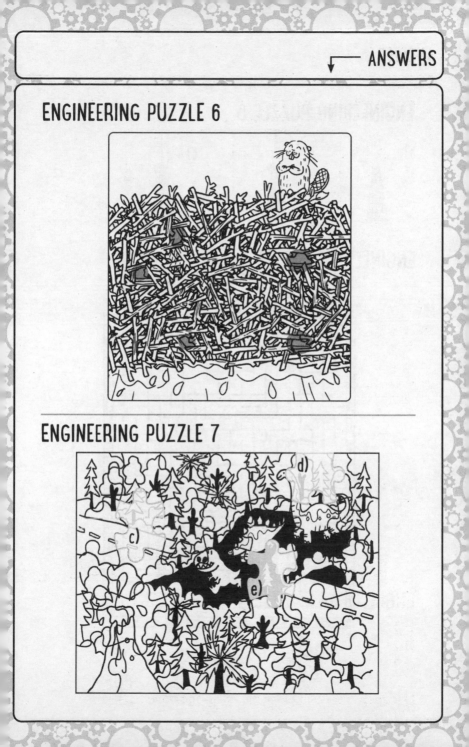

ENGINEERING PUZZLE 7

ENGINEERING PUZZLE 8

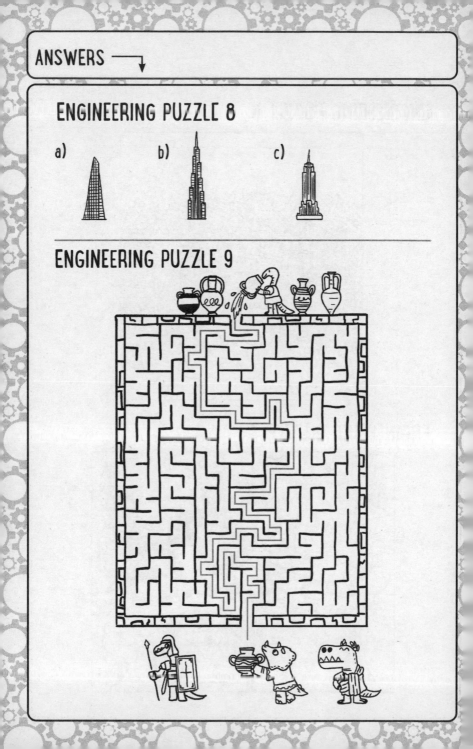

a)

b)

c)

ENGINEERING PUZZLE 9

ENGINEERING PUZZLE 10

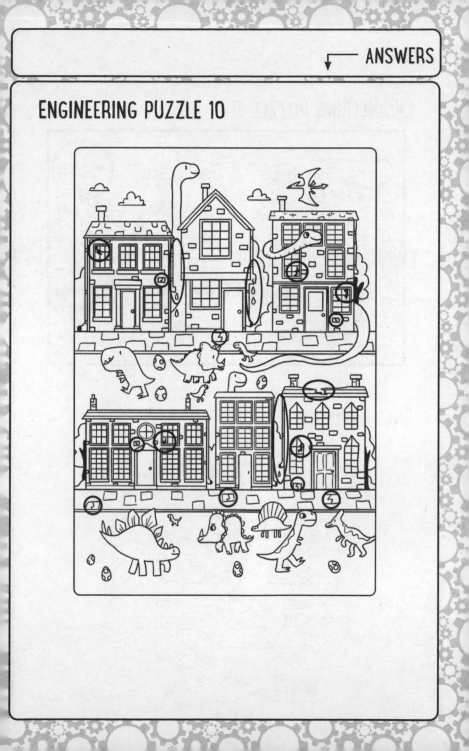

ENGINEERING PUZZLE 11

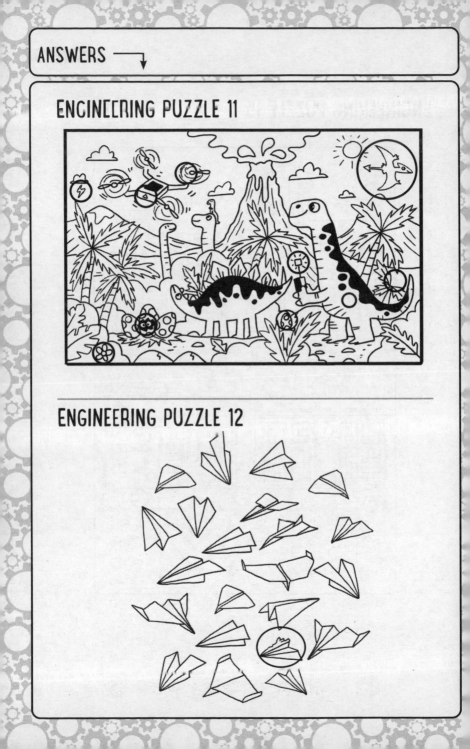

ENGINEERING PUZZLE 12

ENGINEERING PUZZLE 13

d) matches exactly.

ENGINEERING PUZZLE 14

a) 5
b) 6
c) 2
d) 4
e) 3
f) 1

ENGINEERING PUZZLE 15

ENGINEERING PUZZLE 16

She ended up in fourth gear.

ENGINEERING PUZZLE 17

Spike lives in **a)**.

ENGINEERING PUZZLE 18

Bell: 13
Key: 22
Coin: 17

ENGINEERING PUZZLE 19

a) 230 km per hour
b) 278 km per hour
c) 240 km per hour
d) 275 km per hour
e) 290 km per hour (this is the only
one which will be able to take off)

ENGINEERING PUZZLE 20

Ship **a)** can hold Sets **1**, **5**, **6** and **7**.
Ship **b)** can hold Sets **2** and **3**.
Ship **c)** can hold Set **4**.

ENGINEERING PUZZLE 21

ENGINEERING PUZZLE 22

b) *is the matching X-ray.*

ENGINEERING PUZZLE 23

e) *is the lock the key will fit into.*

ENGINEERING PUZZLE 21

ENGINEERING PUZZLE 25

d) can make it the whole way home with his light on.

ENGINEERING PUZZLE 26

a) 2
b) 1
c) 3

MATHS PUZZLE 1

a) 5 (subtract 2 at each step)
b) 56 (add 6 at each step)
c) 121 (add 17 at each step)
d) 1 (divide by 3 at each step)
e) 31 (add 1, 2, 3, 4, 5, etc at each step)

MATHS PUZZLE 2

Albie is 10
Bernie is 8
Chloe is 6

MATHS PUZZLE 3

There are 40 circles in total, made up of 12 at the top-left, 8 at the top-right, 12 at the bottom-right and 8 at the bottom-left. The easiest way to count is to draw over each circle as you count it.

MATHS PUZZLE 4

a)

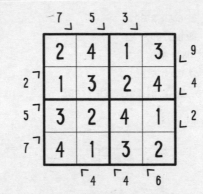

	7⌐	5⌐	3⌐	
	2	4	1	3	⌐ 9
2⌐	1	3	2	4	⌐ 4
5⌐	3	2	4	1	⌐ 2
7⌐	4	1	3	2	
	⌐4	⌐4	⌐6	

b)

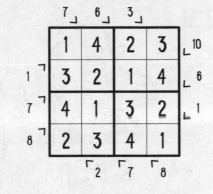

	7⌐	6⌐	3⌐	
	1	4	2	3	⌐ 10
1⌐	3	2	1	4	⌐ 6
7⌐	4	1	3	2	⌐ 1
8⌐	2	3	4	1	
	⌐2	⌐7	⌐8	

MATHS PUZZLE 5

Apple: 4
Banana: 3
Cherry: 6

MATHS PUZZLE 6

a) +11
b) ×4

MATHS PUZZLE 7

a)

4	1	5	6	3	2
6	3	2	4	1	5
3	2	6	1	5	4
5	4	1	2	6	3
2	6	3	5	4	1
1	5	4	3	2	6

b)

5	6	4	1	3	2
3	1	2	5	4	6
4	3	6	2	1	5
2	5	1	3	6	4
6	2	3	4	5	1
1	4	5	6	2	3

MATHS PUZZLE 8

a) 16 = 1 + 7 + 8
b) 28 = 10 + 13 + 5
c) 31 = 10 + 13 + 8

MATHS PUZZLE 9

a) 7
b) 25
c) 30

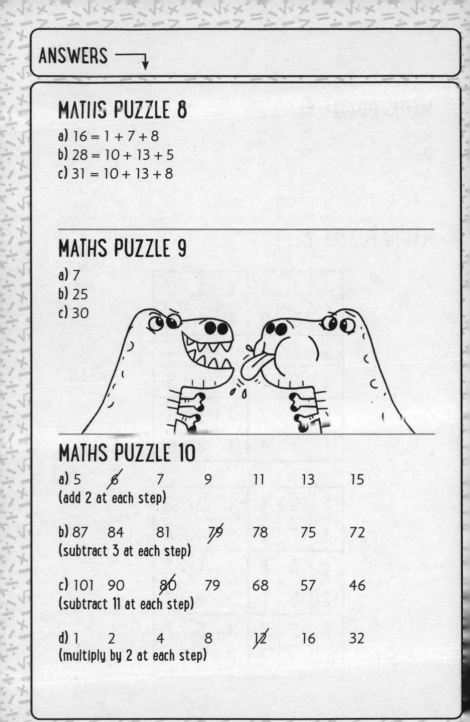

MATHS PUZZLE 10

a) 5   6̸   7   9   11   13   15
(add 2 at each step)

b) 87   84   81   7̸9̸   78   75   72
(subtract 3 at each step)

c) 101   90   8̸0̸   79   68   57   46
(subtract 11 at each step)

d) 1   2   4   8   1̸2̸   16   32
(multiply by 2 at each step)

MATHS PUZZLE 11

a)

	5	5	5	5	
6	2	4	1	3	4
4	3	1	4	2	6
6	4	2	3	1	4
4	1	3	2	4	6
	5	5	5	5	

b)

	5	5	3	7	
4	1	3	2	4	6
6	4	2	1	3	4
6	2	4	3	1	4
4	3	1	4	2	6
	5	5	7	3	

MATHS PUZZLE 12

a)

2	+	4	=	6
+		÷		
3	x	1	=	3
=		=		
5		4		

b)

9	+	7	=	16
x		–		
8	–	6	=	2
=		=		
72		1		

MATIIS PUZZLE 15

The **circle** weighs the **most**.
The **square** weighs the **least**.

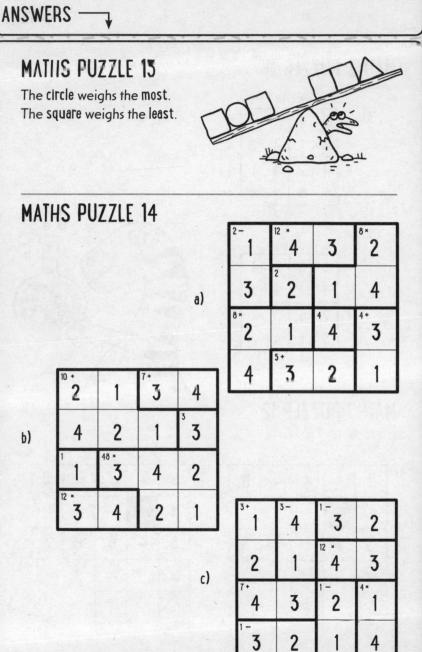

MATHS PUZZLE 14

a)

2− 1	12 × 4	3	8 × 2
3	2 2	1	4
8 × 2	1	4 4	4 + 3
4	5 + 3	2	1

b)

10 + 2	1	7 + 3	4
4	2	1	3 3
1 1	48 × 3	4	2
12 × 3	4	2	1

c)

3 + 1	3 − 4	1 − 3	2
2	1	12 × 4	3
7 + 4	3	1 − 2	4 × 1
1 − 3	2	1	4

MATHS PUZZLE 15

a) 5 coins: 20 + 20 + 20 + 10 + 5
b) 9 coins: 20 + 20 + 10 + 10 + 5 + 5 + 2 + 2 + 1
c) 7 ways: 5+2+1, 5+1+1+1, 2+2+2+2, 2+2+2+1+1,
   2+2+1+1+1+1, 2+1+1+1+1+1+1, 1+1+1+1+1+1+1+1

MATHS PUZZLE 16

a) 18 = 6 + 12
b) 29 = 6 + 11 + 12
c) 34 = 5 + 6 + 11 + 12
d) 42 = 4 + 5 + 10 + 11 + 12

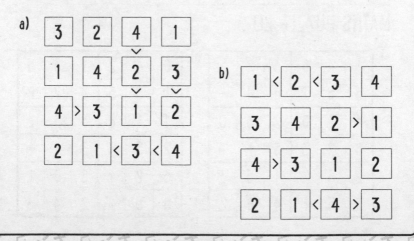

MATHS PUZZLE 17

a)

3	2	4 ˅	1
1	4	2 ˅	3 ˅
4 > 3	1	2
2	1 < 3 < 4

b)

1 <	2 <	3	4
3	4	2 >	1
4 >	3	1	2
2	1 <	4 >	3

MATHS PUZZLE 18

$18 + 20 = 38$
$10 \times 2 = 20$
$15 \times 3 = 45$
$7 \times 5 = 35$
$8 \div 4 = 2$

MATHS PUZZLE 19

a) x4 then -3
b) x5 then -10
c) x3 then -2
d) x2 then -1

MATHS PUZZLE 20

a)

1	4	6	3	2	5
3	5	2	6	4	1
4	1	5	2	3	6
6	2	3	5	1	4
2	6	4	1	5	3
5	3	1	4	6	2

b)

6	4	2	1	3	5
1	3	5	4	2	6
4	1	6	3	5	2
2	5	3	6	1	4
3	2	1	5	6	1
5	6	1	2	4	3

MATHS PUZZLE 21

a) 135 minutes

b) 9am

c) Friday

d) The smallest is 2), since there 5 months with fewer than 31 days (February, April, June, September and November) whereas there are 7 days in a week and there are 8 months with an 'r' in (January, February, March, April, September, October, November and December).

MATHS PUZZLE 22

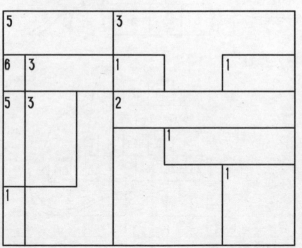

Keep count by working out how many rectangles can be made by each **top-left corner**, as shown above. Then you can add up all the counts to get the final answer, which is **32**.

MATHS PUZZLE 23

a)

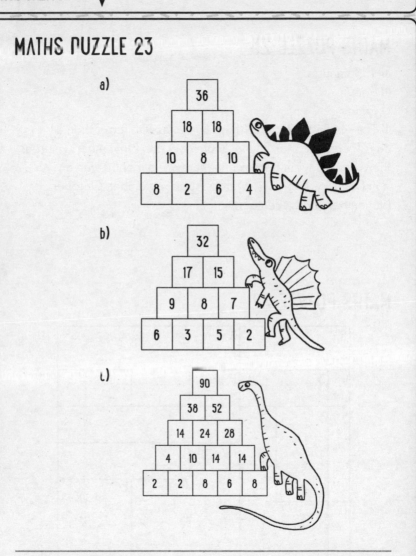

b)

c)

MATHS PUZZLE 24

42 cubes: **6** on the first layer (counting down from the top),
9 on the second layer, **11** on the third layer and **16** on the
fourth layer.

MATHS PUZZLE 25

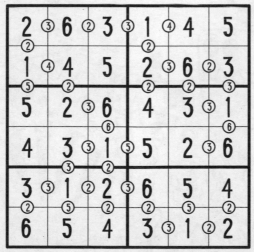

The total is 28.

MATHS PUZZLE 26

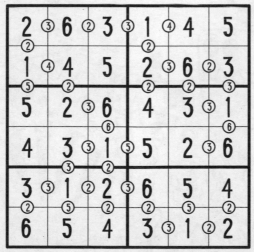

NOTES
AND
SCRIBBLES

NOTES AND SCRIBBLES →

ALSO AVAILABLE:

ISBN 9781780556192

ISBN 9781780556185

ISBN 9781780555638

ISBN 9781780555935

ISBN 9781780555621

ISBN 9781780556628

ISBN 9781780554730

ISBN 9781780554723

ISBN 9781780555409

ISBN 9781780556208

ISBN 9781780553146

ISBN 9781780553078

ISBN 9781780553085

ISBN 9781780552491